I

hope

this

reaches

her in time

good women are tired of giving
their love to people who do nothing
but break their spirit
mighty women are tired of using
their strength to hold on to relationships
that aren't worthy of their energy
these women are capable
of walking away and they will

eventually the girl you took for granted
will take her love and give it to herself
and someday someone better than you
will love her in all the ways
you couldn't

the joy is replaced with sadness
your expectations become disappointment
the truth was just an attractive lie
a bunch of letters forming words
that came together to create sentences
of manipulation

the heart becomes cold
as if to lose it's summer
the soul becomes tired
you and your restless spirit

what's behind those dead eyes
you wear that blank expression
like new skin
you wear sadness like the latest fashion
you wear pain like garments
you've been draped in anguish

don't you miss who you were
before who you became
took over your life
do you miss yourself
like i miss you
do you even remember
what it felt like to be happy
have you forgotten yourself
beneath your troubles

and all of this for a love
that turned out to be hatred
all of this for a heart
that never deserved yours
all of this hurt
for a relationship
that would never work
all of yourself
all of everything
invested into something
that now feels like nothing

drops of rain on windows
the city looks like you
as melancholy fills the streets
the chill in the air
feels like your breath
and the weather resembles
everything that sits within your soul

you are cold
at times numb
you run from the feeling of it all
sometimes you simply walk
but either way it all catches up to you
like darkness consuming light
and you are once more reminded
of all the things you force yourself to forget

aren't you tired of this shit
the constant struggle
the feeling of loneliness
while lying next to the one
who promised to love you
but never kept their word
waiting for change
afraid to accept that
it won't get better

aren't you tired of their shit
the back and forth
not knowing where you stand
the wars, all this fighting
without the feeling of victory
all you've felt is defeat

.

the girl who deserves the sun
is tired of being rained on

the girl you don't appreciate
will get tired of loving you

my generation is filled
with lovers who will never know
the true meaning of love

relationships that feel more
like a prison term
and a happiness
that is simply a delusion

my generation, filled with chaos
no peace, it's difficult, it's complicated
it's nothing, it hurts, it gets worse

you should have loved her
when she cared

you should have tried harder for her

1:11...

one day you'll miss her
one day you'll understand
there will be nights
filled with darkness
and you will look for her light
there will be nights
where sleep will escape you
and your mind will think
of what is gone

she, like memories
will run through your brain
like blood surging through veins
and you'll reach for her hand
then find yourself lost

she could have been
the love of your life
but you refused to love her
she could have been
your soul mate
but i guess you'll never know

and so the loneliness
will grow from the emptiness
you feel
those nights will be the toughest
those mornings, even tougher
it'll hurt, you should have loved her

the pain you feel
will be the same heartache
you put her through
and now you know
you'll finally understand
how much it hurts
to want someone
who doesn't want you

you were the emptiness i felt
you were darkness consuming me
you were the thing
keeping me from happiness

i was the ocean
you wanted rivers
i was the moon
you chased the stars

i needed to find myself
but you were keeping me
from me

the years i spent
losing myself
while trying to keep you

1:11 in the morning
my heart is searching
for a feeling that doesn't hurt

my mind just wants
to think of something
that'll make me smile

my heart breaks with yours
my soul, just as restless
as your own

i fall beside you
i understand your silence
and you are not alone

you deserve so much more
than what you've been given
you owe it to yourself
to give yourself the love
that you've misplaced in others

you are more than just a body count
you are more than just a conquest
you are more than just a name
on the list of hearts
they took advantage of

and even after it happens
you will always be more
than they deserved

we find time to waste
remembering the faces
we struggle to erase

we give energy to those
who give nothing in return

we learn the hard way
but instead of letting go
we stay

we love
we fall in love
with relationships
filled with hate

we become content
with giving ourselves
to the wrong mate

crashing into walls
worsening our wounds
deepening the bruises

the endless cycle
of recycling relationships
that no longer deserve
our attention

being attentive
to lovers
who pretend to care

constantly showing up
for others
who are never there

you are chained
to the past
it's time to free yourself

it's almost as if
her soul is a pack of wolves
she's brave, she's strong
she's unstoppable

you can miss people
but you don't have to
want them back

you can forgive people
but you don't have to
give them second chances

121914

she made oceans
with her tears
she used the heartache
as motivation to build
the boat
in hopes of sailing
far away from everything
and everyone
who hurt her

the moon is watching you
it hears your sighs
it witnesses your struggles
to close your eyes

she wore loneliness
in a smile
she hid the sadness
with laughter

the clouds dance around each other
like lovers avoiding the truth

all of her stars are burning

cry
empty yourself
of all the pain
he caused you

i was killing me
to give us life
i was drowning
to save the person
who kept pushing my head
under water

your absence taught me
how to be my own lover

you will be ready
when it is time
for your heart
to fight back
against the one
who hurt you

girls like you have roses
inside of them
that are strong enough
to bloom through blizzards

you began as roots
but you blossom into more
you are not your past
be here, be present
be more

relationships end
but your story mustn't finish

someday your soul will no longer linger
in places where pain exist

i won't judge you
or criticize you
for doing what you've done

i only wish you saw
what i see when i look at you
i only wish you wished for more
than what you've settled for

you are not a phase
you are not some trend
you are more than just something
to do for the moment
more than a hobby
more than you may even know

you are more
and you deserve more
than what they're willing
to give you

you, reading this
your eyes dancing
on this page
you, the one who knows
how it feels
to have their heart
racing out of their chest
overrun with anxicty
desperate for relief

it is you who wants to be loved
understood for everything that you are
it is you, the one reading this
the one who is close to tears
so close to breaking

it is you who will save yourself
because this is what you've always done
because you are strong enough
to do so

there are so many wars
going on at night
so many hearts are fighting
to survive without light

the darkness contains
everything we should forget
the regrets are magnified
the night is plagued with what ifs

dancing to the silence of the night
we sway like a bed of roses in the wind

he only loved you
in the dark
in secret
behind closed bedroom doors

he was yours
until he came
and then he left
whenever he was done
draining you of everything
he never deserved

aren't you tired of a love
that feels less than everything
you claimed you wanted
has your soul grown weary
of being with someone
who only wants you
for a nut
someone who cums
but never stays

your heart deserves better

i was standing here
the whole time
my heart in my hand
prepared for commitment
and eager to love
but you didn't see me
until after it failed with the others
and i decided not to be
your second choice
your last ditch effort at love

i refused to be the one you chose
after the ones you overlooked me for
refused to choose you

i was standing here the whole time
but you decided not to see me

maybe the bad boys
aren't good enough for you

it was raining in the park that day
she was sitting on a bench
mid may, wearing the eyes of sadness
and for the life of me
i couldn't tell if she was crying
because her tears
would have blended in
with the rain
her soul as dark as the afternoon sky
and i said nothing
but wondered why
the girl sitting alone
hand clutching her phone
at a loss for words
with so much pain in her heart

thought it was royal
but all i see is fake kings
claiming a throne
they don't deserve to sit on
reaching for a crown
they don't deserve to wear

he calls but mostly when he needs something
haven't you noticed
pretending to give a damn
about your day just to get his way

the manipulation hurts
but you'll sit there and make excuses
for him
seeing what you want
hearing one thing and thinking another
whatever helps with the delusional
because the truth
is so much harder to accept

foolish of me
to believe
that a dysfunctional family
could function in a way
that made me feel loved

just like any and everything else
things are never what they seem
people change or maybe they simply
revert back to everything they're supposed to be

you mean to tell me
that you're so afraid
of being alone
that you've decided
to hold on to the one person
who makes you feel lonely
even while sitting beside them

you keep saying you want
real love and yet you've chosen
to entertain the same person
who will never love you

the heart wants
what it wants
and it's too bad
that the heart
your heart
doesn't want
the one who deserves you

i'd tell you to let go
but you'll just say
it's easier said than done

typical
predictable
claiming to be in love
with someone who has done nothing
to make you feel loved
someone who has done nothing
but make you hate yourself
and sometimes you hate them
just the same

i wish your desire
to be happy
somehow outweighed
your tolerance for the heartache
they've caused you

are we still pretending
that it doesn't hurt
holding on to broken relationships
in hopes that some day they'll work

are we still holding on
using the last bit of strength
we have
on lovers who only wish to use us up
then toss us out like a piece of notebook
filled with errors

are we still listening to lies
believing in liars who say whatever
they need to say
just to get another opportunity
to hurt us

are we hurting yet saying nothing
it's painful but we've kept quiet
in hopes that things will change

are we...
are you...
am i...

your father
the first man you knew
the first man you'd love
one half of the reason why
you grew up so hard

so young and yet
your heart began to ache
breaking into a million pieces
as you alone would learn
to pick yourself up

your father
the first man to disappoint you
the first man to let you down
the first man to cause you
to lower your expectations

he loved you, yes
but i guess not enough
to protect you
while you loved him enough
to look past his failures

you'd go on to accept
his half ass efforts to love you
you'd go on to accept men
and their half ass efforts to love you

your father
only present just enough
for you to feel like you mattered
your lovers
only present enough
to fool you into thinking they cared

i used to wonder to myself
how could you ever love a man
who barely made an effort
but then i witnessed your father
as he barely tried
and with tears in your eyes
you said you loved him

your father taught you
how to love men
who reminded you of him

the broken girls
are the flowers of the earth
they grow through tough conditions
they bloom for themselves

a man child will love you quietly
but a real man will be loud
in his appreciation of your heart

i hope your flowers bloom
through the rain

you don't even see
how often the stars
perform for you
in the middle of every night

the heartache will teach you
then peace will fill you

broken girls
blossom into warriors

beneath a jacket
two sizes larger
than your body
your arms folded
as if to keep your secret

you hid yourself
from the world
because the world betrayed you

the robbing of your innocence
an inappropriate touch

behind those walls
behind the barriers
that keep the world
from your heart
is a woman worth
fighting for

behind those walls
that tall, strong
separation from the world
lives a love worth
wishing for

you are greater
than what has happened
you are far more greater
than the what occurred
in your past

behind those walls
behinds that cement
that has kept others
from hurting you
like the ones from before
lives a love
that only you can provide
a love like yours
is worth climbing the wall
that sits in front
of your heart

what we love
should inspire us
who we love
should inspire
our strength

but you have fallen
for hands
not worthy of your skin
you have fallen for a mind
that will never understand
your value
you have fallen for a heart
incapable of loving you
the way you need

what we love
what you love
should feel like paradise
during the storm

the person you love
should feel like stillness
during an earthquake

but you've fallen
for someone
who will never be able
to be brave enough
to fall for you

the night will fade away
and so will the darkness
the moon will float into the abyss
and the sun will announce itself
with a ray of light and hope
and warmth and beauty

the morning will come
the day will begin
and the corners of my room
the dark corners of my room
will be filled with a light
that will kill off
all the things
and all the pain that haunts me
during the rising of the moon

the sun will sit in the sky
and it will shine
providing it's light
giving me enough time
and a peace of mind
to evade you

because you live in the midnights
where i feel hopeless
filled with despair

you live in the night
the darkness, the restlessness
the air of uncertainty

you live in the moments
where my eyes cannot close
you survive in shattered dreams
and the bruising of my soul

but just like the night
you fade behind the horizon
and just like the sun
i rise, possibly brighter
and stronger than before

the morning will come
the day will begin
and you will be forgotten
once more

miss me
like archers with bad aim
lose me
like hands on a rope
incapable of holding on

regret leaving me
like the sun
does the sky

my absence
like a slow death
that you'll struggle to survive

look for me
like eyes struggling
through darkness

reach for me
like lungs struggling
for air

search for me
like the meaning of words
search for me where you left me
and i will no longer be there

telling her that she's beautiful
while destroying her confidence is abuse

telling her you love her
while acting as if you hate her
is abuse

filling her up with false hope
with no intention of changing
or doing better is abuse

until next time, talk to you soon…
(call ends…)